Thank you to my husband, Steve Sexauer, for your love and your generous assistance.

Thank you to my family and friends. I am grateful for your support and your feedback.

IN LOVING MEMORY OF STEILYN GRAY MARTIN

FEBRUARY 1, 1981 – JUNE 23, 2016

<u>The Sleepover</u>
A Steilyn Story
Copyright © by Molly Kathleen Martin
Printed by CreateSpace, An Amazon.com Company
Charleston, SC

For author information, contact: mollykathleenmartin@gmail.com
Website: www.steilynstories.com

All rights reserved.

ISBN-3: 978-1722375560
ISBN-10: 1722375566

The Sleepover

A Steilyn Story

Story by Molly K. Martin

Drawings by Emma Fore

Steilyn's cousin, Ben, is spending the night! The boys are busy arranging their sleeping bags for the sleepover.

Steilyn's mom is in the kitchen fixing dinner. Her speciality – pizza burgers, applesauce and chocolate ice cream for dessert!

.

The dogs, Buddy and Beauregard, run into the kitchen to beg for food. They jump up on the boys. Steilyn and Ben try their best to keep the dogs out of the kitchen.

Then, **Woof!**

The dogs see a squirrel in the yard. They bark loudly to be let outside!

After dinner the boys eagerly prepare to watch their favorite movies.

The movies will provide plenty of giggles for the night!

The dogs are happy to be on the couch. They love being with Steilyn and Ben in the TV room.

At midnight, Steilyn's mom turns off the TV and says, "Try to get some sleep, boys."

Buddy and Beauregard shuffle off to the living room to snuggle into their favorite chairs.

The boys are too excited to sleep. They talk softly about their plans for the next day. Suddenly, Steilyn whispers, "Sshhh. Did you hear that?"

"Yeah, I hear talking," says Ben.

The boys stay still and listen quietly. They hear low, raspy voices coming from the living room!

Curious, the boys crawl army style toward the living room. They stop at the doorway and listen. They hear talking!

"Buddy, I've had it with stupid milk bones." mutters Beauregard. "We need a plan to get the good treats that taste like bacon."

"Yeah, Steilyn and Ben had pizza burgers," says Buddy in a low voice. "Milk bones taste like cardboard."

The boys soon realize that the dogs are talking!

Steilyn and Ben creep further into the living room.

The boys overhear Buddy and Beauregard making plans to get the good treats from the kitchen!

"Buddy, the good treats are on the kitchen counter. I can reach them if I climb on your back," says Beauregard.

"Ok, let's get 'em," mumbles Buddy.

The dogs make their way to the kitchen.

Steilyn and Ben grab each dog as they enter into the kitchen and exclaim, "Hey, we heard you talking! When did you learn to talk!"

Puzzled, Buddy and Beauregard look at the boys and think, "Don't you know dogs can't talk!"

In the kitchen, Steilyn tells the dogs to sit. He gives each dog the good treats that taste like bacon.

"OK, guys, let's hear you talk again," urges Steilyn.

Buddy and Beauregard remain silent. They quietly stare at the boys.

"Come on, guys," pleads Steilyn. "We heard you talking just a minute ago."

Buddy and Beauregard look silently at the boys. They are hoping for more good treats.

"Darn, no more good treats." With that thought, Buddy and Beauregard walk back to the living room and their favorite chairs.

Steilyn and Ben return to their sleeping bags. They shake their heads in disbelief.

They cannot believe what just occurred.

The boys crawl into their sleeping bags to settle in for the night.

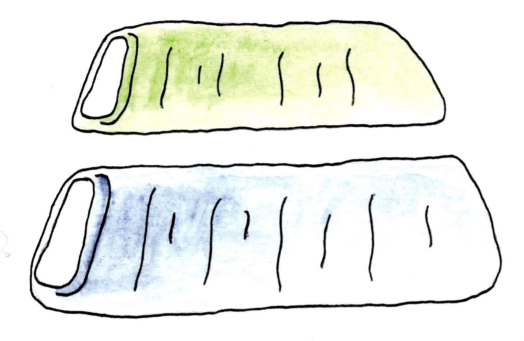

Still confused by what just happened, Steilyn and Ben stare at each other.

"We heard them talking, right?" asks Steilyn.

"Yep," retorts Ben, "but we know that dogs cannot talk."

"True," says Steilyn, "but I know what I heard."

Do you wonder if dogs talk at night?

THE END!

We hope you enjoyed "The Sleepover".

To read more about the characters in the book, please see the following pages.

The talking dogs! The real Buddy and Beauregard.

<u>A Special Note about Beauregard</u>: Sometimes kids and grownups do not know how to say Beauregard's name. When that happens, they will re-name him! A few examples of new names for Beauregard from our readers are "Bogart" and "Burgerdog" and "Bow"! Please feel free to make up your own name. Beauregard will love you no matter what name you use!

About Buddy and Beauregard

Buddy was dropped off at a Humane Society in Missouri by the family that raised him from a puppy. After a couple of years, the family decided that they did not want him anymore. So…Buddy went from living with a mom, a dad and their three children to living in a "cage". The Humane Society worked hard to make sure Buddy found another home. Buddy was adopted on November 26, 2005 by Steve and Molly.

Beauregard was found wandering in Southeastern Missouri. He was taken to a nearby Humane Society. They gave Beauregard medicine and lots of love. When Beauregard trotted, he would often hold his back, left leg off the ground. He had muscle damage. Once Beauregard was feeling better, the Humane Society looked for a family that would adopt him. He was adopted on December 13, 2008 by Steve and Molly.

Buddy and Beauregard also have a sister, Lizzy, who was adopted on October 14, 2006. Buddy, Beauregard and Lizzy bring much love and joy to Steve and Molly. Oh, and Beauregard's left leg is much better from all the play time he has with his forever family!

BEN

Ben is one of Steilyn's many cousins and a best friend. One of the bedrooms at Steilyn's home is named "Ben's Room" depicting the many nights Ben stayed over!

Ben is happily married to Kate. The November after Steilyn's death in June of 2016, Ben and Kate welcomed their first child, a son whom they named Jackson Steilyn Martin. What a blessing and a tribute to Steilyn!

Ben and Kate live in California where Ben is on active duty with the Coast Guard. Kate works from home for a company located in Chicago, Illinois.

"The Sleepover" is dedicated to Jackson Steilyn Martin

Steilyn and Stacey (Harrison) – married 10/3/2015

Steilyn's humor, loyalty and respect for others are what made him a special person. The "Steilyn Story Series" uses art, photos and fun adventures to celebrate Steilyn and his cousins.

Buddy, Beauregard and Lizzy

Jackson Steilyn Martin

Steilyn and Ben

A Steilyn favorite: Pizza Burgers!

Ingredients: A pound of hamburger, a package of hamburger buns, mozzarella cheese squares, one 15 ounce can of pizza sauce and butter or margarine.

- Brown the hamburger.
- Add the pizza sauce and stir.
- Butter 4 hamburger bun halves (tops or the bottoms) and place on a cookie tray. Broil the buns until the butter has melted.
- Scoop the hamburger/pizza sauce mix (it should be warm from the stove) onto each half bun.
- Place one mozzarella square on top of the hamburger/pizza sauce mix.
- Put the tray with the buns back into the oven to broil until the cheese has melted.
- Serve "open face" (no need to put a bun on top!).

Emma Fore

When I began planning a tribute to Steilyn and his cousins in the way of a children's book, I reached out to our neighbor, Carla Hoyt. I needed someone to do the illustrations. Carla quickly recommended her daughter's friend, Emma Fore. Emma, then a senior in high school, wholeheartedly agreed to help with my project.

Emma is a treasure. She is a brilliant student of math and loves drawing. This was her first try with caricature drawing. I am so appreciative of Emma, her hard work and her talent!

A group of third graders from the Pocahontas Elementary School in Pocahontas, Illinois, reacted to Emma's illustrations with this comment, "She is a really good drawer!" Yes. She is.

Molly K. Martin

Made in the USA
Monee, IL
07 February 2023